*How We Elected Lincoln*

Mr. Lincoln on horseback in front of his residence, Springfield, Illinois, at the time of his return from the campaign with Senator Douglas. [*From an old Print.*]

# *How We Elected Lincoln*

## Personal Recollections

ABRAM J. DITTENHOEFER

Foreword by Kathleen Hall Jamieson

**PENN**

University of Pennsylvania Press

Philadelphia

Originally published 1916 by Harper & Brothers
Foreword copyright © 2005 University of Pennsylvania Press
All rights reserved

Printed in the United States of America on acid-free paper

10   9   8   7   6   5   4   3   2   1

Paperback edition first published 2005 by
University of Pennsylvania Press
Philadelphia, Pennsylvania 19104–4011

Library of Congress Cataloging-in-Publication Data

Dittenhoefer, Abram J. (Abram Jesse), 1836–1919.
    How we elected Lincoln : personal recollections / Abram J.
Dittenhoefer ; foreword by Kathleen Hall Jamieson.
        p.   cm.
    ISBN: 0-8122-1914-7 (pbk. : alk. paper)
    Originally published: New York : Harper & Brothers, 1916. With
new foreword.
    Includes bibliographical references.
    1. Lincoln, Abraham, 1809–1865—Anecdotes.   2. Dittenhoefer,
Abram J. (Abram Jesse), 1836–1919—Anecdotes.   3. Lincoln,
Abraham, 1809–1865—Friends and associates—Anecdotes.
4. Presidents—United States—Election—1860—Anecdotes.
5. Presidents—United States—Election—1864—Anecdotes.
5. Political campaigns—United States—History—19th century—
Anecdotes.   6. United States—Politics and government—1861–
1865—Anecdotes.   I. Title.   II. Jamieson, Kathleen Hall
E457.15 .D6   2005
324.973′068—dc 22                                        2005042023

# Contents

# Foreword

KATHLEEN HALL JAMIESON

Just after the election of 1856, the Supreme Court, in the *Dred Scott* case, stepped into an ongoing Congressional debate to rule that Congress could not bar slavery in the territories. Nor, said the decision, could the legislatures in the territories themselves. The year before the election of 1860, John Brown's attempt to inspire a slave rebellion led to his execution.

In 1860 there were four major candidates for president: Abraham Lincoln, heading the Republican ticket; Stephen A. Douglas, the champion of the popular sovereignty Democrats; John Bell, of the Constitutional Party; and John C. Breckinridge, the nominee of the Southern Democrats.

Breckinridge favored protecting slavery in the territories. The contest came down to Lincoln versus Breckinridge, South versus North and West. Indeed, Lincoln and his running mate Hannibal Hamlin did not even appear on ballots in the South.

After a bitter election Abraham Lincoln won the Electoral College decisively by carrying the states of the West and North. But, taken together, the three other contenders garnered a larger popular vote than did "the Rail Splitter" from Illinois. The composition of the vote forecast the future. Here was a nation divided by region. Eighteen slave-free states supported Lincoln; eleven slave states backed Breckinridge. Douglas, who memorably had debated Lincoln over slavery and union in their earlier contest for the Senate, received only 12 electoral votes. In December 1860, after the ballots had been cast but before Lincoln had been officially notified of his election, South Carolina seceded from the union. The *Charleston Mercury*'s headline declared on December 20 of that year, "The Union Is Dissolved."[1] Other states followed.

On February 26, 1861, Abraham Lincoln replied to the Committee of Congress reporting the Electoral Count by writing "with deep gratitude to my countrymen for this mark of their confidence; with a distrust of my own ability to perform the required duty under the most favorable circumstances, now rendered doubly difficult by existing national perils; yet with a firm reliance on the strength of our free government, and the ultimate loyalty of the people to the just principles upon which it is founded, and above all an unshaken trust in the Supreme Ruler of the nations, I accept this trust."[2]

In his March 4, 1861, inaugural address Lincoln declared, "In your hands, my dissatisfied fellow countrymen, and not in mine, is the momentous issue of civil war. . . . You have no oath registered in heaven to destroy the Government, while I shall have the most solemn one to 'PRESERVE, PROTECT, AND DEFEND IT.'" Fortunately for Lincoln, the mass audience was far more likely to read his words than hear them. Until the advent of radio more than a half century later, political speech created its impact when it was read by the public in newspapers. Of the first inaugural, one observer noted, "Mr. Lincoln was pale and very nervous, and did not read his address very well. His spectacles troubled him, his position was crowded and uncomfortable, and, in short, nothing has been done to render the performance of this great duty either dignified in effect or, physically speaking, easy for the President. The great crowd in the grounds behaved very well, but manifested little or no enthusiasm."[3] Then, as now, impressions of politics are shaped by partisan predispositions. In *How We Elected Lincoln*, Lincoln enthusiast Abram Dittenhoefer recalls instead, "The President impressed me as being serious in manner. His voice sounded shrill, but he was talking at high pitch in order that he might be heard by as many as possible of the immense crowd. Little by little his auditors warmed toward him, until finally the applause became overwhelming, spontaneous, and enthusiastic. Then, for the first time, it dawned on me that Lincoln . . . [was] one of the few great men of all times; and I may say safely that my conviction was shared by all within hearing of his voice" (pp. 49–50). Little more than a month later, on April 12, 1861, the Confederates fired the first rocket on the Union's Fort Sumter. Barely four years later, on April 14, 1865, Lincoln was shot.

Abram J. Dittenhoefer's *How We Elected Lincoln* is a first-hand account of the campaigns that twice secured the presidency for Lincoln. Known as a "Southerner with Northern principles" (p. 1), Dittenhoefer's account testifies to the importance of rhetoric in the country's conflict over slavery. "My convictions were irrevocably changed," he writes, "by reading of [Ohio Senator Benjamin F.] Wade's speech" (pp. 4–5).

Although more a testament to Lincoln's greatness than a dispassionate account, the book provides a window on the process of electing and reelecting a president a century and a half ago. "Fraudulent voting prevailed to a large extent" (p. 4). Marching clubs, known as "Wide Awakes," paraded through towns. Candidates' biographies were reduced to identifying labels. "The appellation of Pathfinder was given to [Gen. John C.] Fremont because in earlier years he had explored the then hardly known Western territory, with the aid of scouts and pioneers, and had indicated passes and routes through the mountains" (p. 6). Slogans abounded. " 'Free Speech, Free Soil, Free Men, and Fremont!' These words were shouted at all public meetings and in all public processions." Then, as now, slogans digested the central message of a campaign. "Indeed the [Fremont] cry was a stump speech in itself" (p. 7). The link between electioneering and entertainment was strong, with barbecues being "the usual accompaniment of a political campaign" (p. 7). Money mattered as well. "It is doubtful if the National Committee had more than $100,000 to spend, and most of this went for printing and postage. . . . Had it been necessary for Mr. Lincoln or his managers to raise a half-million dollars, or go down to defeat, Lincoln would have lost out" (p. 39).

Change the names, update the language, and Dittenhoefer's complaints about attacks by the other side and by the partisan press sound remarkably current. "Denunciation of Lincoln by Democratic spellbinders was of the bitterest character. Newspapers affiliated with the antiwar party criticized every act of the administration and belittled the conduct of the war by Federal generals in the field" (p. 92). So, too, do accusations of pandering. "The great Daniel Webster had ruined his political career some years previously by trying to be 'all things to all men' politically" (p. 19).

Then, as now, candidates offered subtle and obvious allusions to their religious faith. "Lincoln was fond of quoting from the Bible without mentioning the fact, whereas Douglas was often caught differing with the Scriptures. Naturally Lincoln took advantage of his political opponent's lack of Biblical knowledge" (p. 11).

The corruption of the system that concerns us has parallels in the past as well. So, for example, Dittenhoefer decries the presence of "commercial grafters and alleged statesmen, every one of whom was in politics for personal profit" (p. 69).

In sum, this admiring account of the political campaigns and presidency of Abraham Lincoln is a useful window on a consequential time in the nation's history and a helpful confirmation of how the process by which we elect a president has changed and how it has remained the same.

*Notes*

1.  Oliver Gramling, *AP: The Story of News* (New York: Farrar and Rinehart, 1940), p. 37.

2.  Reprinted in *The Collected Works of Abraham Lincoln*, vol. 4, ed. Roy P. Basler (New Brunswick, N.J.: Rutgers University Press, 1953), p. 246.

3.  Carl Sandburg, *Abraham Lincoln: The War Years*, 4 vols. (New York: Harcourt, Brace and World, 1939), 1, p. 123.

# Preface

This book offers my personal recollections of the immortal Emancipator, and of the memorable campaigns of 1860 and 1864, in which, as a young man, I was actively engaged.

In looking back upon a life of fourscore years I find no prouder memories than those of the years 1860–65. They illumined my being, and my life became inspired through association with the immortal Abraham Lincoln and the great men of the anti-slavery conflict.

I am unwilling to allow these reminiscences to go forth without giving credit to my old friend Julius Chambers, for the valuable assistance he rendered in compiling them.

*How We Elected Lincoln*

# I
# The Man—Lincoln

Circumstances brought to me personal knowledge of Mr. Lincoln for nearly four years. I had frequent interviews with him, and so was able to form a well-considered estimate of the great Emancipator's character and personality.

Born in Charleston, South Carolina, of Democratic pro-slavery parents, I was brought in early youth to New York; and although imbued with the sentiments and antipathies of my Southern environment, I soon became known as a Southerner with Northern principles. At that time there were many Northern men with Southern principles.

The city of New York, as I discovered upon reaching the age of observation, was virtually an annex of the South, the New York merchants having extensive and very profitable business relations with the merchants south of the Mason and Dixon line.

The South was the best customer of New York. I

often said in those days, "Our merchants have for sale on their shelves their principles, together with their merchandise."

An amusing incident occurred to my knowledge which aptly illustrates the condition of things in this pro-slavery city. A Southerner came to a New York merchant, who was a dealer in brushes and toilet articles, and offered him a large order for combs. The New York merchant, as it happened, was a Quaker, but this was not known to the Southerner. The latter made it a condition, in giving this large order, that the Quaker merchant should exert all his influence in favor of the South. The Southerner wished to do something to offset the great agitation headed by the abolitionists which had been going on for years in the North for the extinction of slavery in the South. The Quaker merchant coolly replied that the South would have to go lousy for a long time before he would sell his combs to them under any such conditions.

Another occurrence that took place at an earlier period still further illumines this intense pro-slavery feeling. When Wendell Phillips, to my mind one of the greatest orators of America, delivered a radical and brilliant anti-slavery speech at the old Tabernacle, situated in Broadway below Canal Street, the hall was filled with pro-slavery shouters; they rotten-egged Phillips in the course of his address. With some friends I was present and witnessed this performance.

At nineteen I was wavering in my fidelity to the principles of the Democratic party, which, in the city of New York, was largely in favor of slavery.

I had just graduated from Columbia College, which was then situated in what is now known as College Place, between Chambers and Murray streets. At that time many of our prominent and wealthy families lived in Chambers, Murray, and Warren streets, and I frequently attended festivities held by the parents of the college boys in the old-fashioned mansions which lined those thoroughfares.

Soon after leaving college I became a student in the law office of Benedict & Boardman, occupying offices in Dey Street, near Broadway. At that time the late John E. Parsons, a distinguished member of the New York bar, was the managing clerk; and Charles O'Connor, the head of the New York bar in that generation, and who, in later years, ran as an Independent candidate for the Presidency, was connected with that firm as counsel.

Sitting one day at my desk, I took up a newspaper, and the debate between Judah P. Benjamin, the rabid but eloquent pro-slavery Senator from Louisiana, and Benjamin F. Wade, the free-soil Senator from Ohio, attracted my attention.

Benjamin had made a strong address in defense of slavery when Wade arose and replied. He began his reply with some bitter and memorable words, words which completely changed my political views.

"I have listened with intense interest," said he, "as I always do to the eloquent speech of my friend, the Senator from Louisiana—an Israelite with Egyptian principles."

My father, who was a prominent merchant of New York in those days, and very influential with the German population, had urged me to become a Democrat, warning me that a public career, if I joined the Republican party, would be impossible in the city of New York. I felt that he was right in that view, as the party was in a hopeless minority, without apparent prospect of ever being able to elect its candidates.

This was absolutely plain from the fact that Tammany Hall controlled the entire election machinery in this city, there being no law at that time which required the registration of voters before Election Day. Moreover, the inspectors of election were Tammany heelers, without any Republican representation on the election boards. In consequence, fraudulent voting prevailed to a large extent.

And yet my convictions were irrevocably changed

by the reading of Wade's speech in answer to Benjamin. It struck me with great force that the Israelite Benjamin, whose ancestors were enslaved in Egypt, ought not to uphold slavery in free America, and could not do so without bringing disgrace upon himself.

Having convinced my father that slavery should no longer be tolerated, he abandoned his old political association, cast his vote for Lincoln and Hamlin, and remained a Republican until his death.

Several years later, if I may anticipate, William M. Tweed, who had not yet become "Boss," but who had great and powerful influence in Tammany Hall, besought me to join Tammany, calling my attention to the fact that the power of the Democratic party was supreme in the city of New York, and that the organization needed some one to influence the German element.

He gave me his assurance that if I came into Tammany Hall I should receive prompt recognition, and in a few years undoubtedly would become judge of the Supreme Court; later on I might go still higher up. I thanked Mr. Tweed for his friendly interest in me, but told him that no political preferment could induce me to abandon my convictions and lead me to support slavery.

When Tweed became the absolute "Boss" of

Tammany, some years later, he renewed his request that I should join Tammany Hall. Recurring to his previous promise, he again urged me to become a member of his organization; again I refused.

One can hardly appreciate to-day what it meant to me, a young man beginning his career in New York, to ally myself with the Republican party. By doing so, not only did I cast aside all apparent hope of public preferment, but I also subjected myself to obloquy from and ostracism by my acquaintances, my clients, and even members of my own family.

I was about twenty years of age when the first Republican convention met at Pittsburg. It succeeded the disruption of the old Whig party, the latter losing in public esteem on account of its indifference toward the slavery question.

Gen. John C. Fremont, known as the Pathfinder, was nominated for President, and William L. Dayton, of New Jersey, was nominated for Vice-President. The appellation of Pathfinder was given to Fremont because in earlier years he had explored the then hardly known Western territory, was the aid of scouts and pioneers, and had indicated passes and routes through the mountains.

Though not yet of age, I stumped for Fremont and Dayton, making many speeches during that memorable campaign, and participating in several barbecues, which were then the usual accompaniment of a political campaign. I was well received in the towns where I was scheduled to speak. A military band and a citizens' committee generally met me at the station, and escorted me through the streets to the hotel or private house in which it was arranged that I should stay.

The thrilling battle-cry of that campaign was, "Free Speech, Free Soil, Free Men, and Fremont!" These words were shouted at all public meetings and in all public processions, and were received with the wildest enthusiasm. Indeed, the cry was a stump speech in itself; it still thrills me as I write. Like the "Marseillaise," it was a shout for freedom set to music.

Fremont had served by appointment for a brief period as Senator from the State of California. His popularity as a candidate was aided by the fact that his wife, Jessie Benton Fremont, was the brilliant daughter of Thomas H. Benton, who for thirty years was a Senator from Missouri; and who, in later years, published his well-known book, *Thirty Years in the United States Senate.* In the later part of his career, Benton, who had been a strong supporter of the "peculiar institution" in the South, became an opponent of the extension of slavery in new territory. Mrs. Fremont was an important figure in that campaign; her name was always mentioned with great respect by the opposition speakers.

Early in the Civil War, President Lincoln, in appreciation of Fremont's splendid services in the exploration of the West and because he had been the first Republican candidate for President, appointed him commander of a portion of the Federal forces. On August 31, 1861, Fremont issued a military order emancipating the slaves of all persons in arms against the United States. This action did not meet with Mr. Lincoln's approval; he considered it premature, and perhaps he was right in that view; accordingly he directed that the proclamation should be withdrawn.

I was afterward reconciled to Fremont's defeat in 1856, for the reason that, had he been elected, the probability is that Abraham Lincoln, the greatest figure in American history, never would have attained the Presidency.

Here it may be of interest to record that in the convention of 1856, which nominated Fremont, Lincoln received one hundred and ten votes for the Vice-presidency, while Mr. Dayton, the successful candidate, had only a few more votes. Nevertheless, Lincoln did not achieve a national reputation until he engaged in the memorable Lincoln and Douglas debates in Illinois.

During the Fremont campaign I sometimes spoke in German, especially in towns in which there was a large Teutonic population, and I was hoping that I might influence the German population of New York, two-thirds of which had allied itself with the Democratic party.

The most memorable event in Mr. Lincoln's career, after the Fremont campaign, was his appearance in joint debate with Stephen A. Douglas, then known as the "Little Giant," during the months of August, September, and October, 1858. The challenge came from Lincoln, in a letter of July 24th, proposing the joint meetings. Seven debates were subsequently agreed upon to take place in Ottawa, Freeport, Jonesboro, Charleston, Galesburg, Quincy, and Alton. These debates attracted great attention in all parts of the country, and were fully reported by the New York and Chicago newspapers. Robert H. Hitt, who afterward became chargé d'affaires at Paris, and in later years chairman of the House Committee on Foreign Affairs, reported stenographically all the speeches, and gave me a vivid impression of them.

In the opening address at Ottawa, the "Little Giant" explained clearly what he meant by the doctrine of popular sovereignty, which he had advocated in the United States Senate for many years, and which by the Free Soil people of the

North was looked upon as merely a blind to cover the extension of slavery in free territory.

Douglas had introduced bills giving Statehood to the Territories of Kansas and Nebraska, and commenting upon these bills he said it was not intended to legislate slavery into any State or Territory or to exclude it therefrom, but "to leave the people thereof entirely free to form and regulate their domestic institutions as they thought best, subject only to the Federal Constitution."

Now in the North the agitation to prevent the extension of slavery in those States was intense; indeed, as the question involved the repeal of the Missouri Compromise, which prohibited the extension of slavery in newly acquired territory and which had been on the statute-book for many years, it became the great issue of the Republican party.

Mr. Lincoln's speeches were filled with quaint phrases and interpolated jests. The latter always were apt and calculated to keep his hearers, friendly or antagonistic, in a good humor. In his Ottawa answer to Douglas's opening speech Mr. Lincoln asserted that any attempt to show that he (Lincoln) advocated "perfect social and political equality between the negro and the white man is only a specious and fantastic arrangement of words, by which one might prove a horse-chestnut was a chestnut horse."

All Lincoln demanded for the negro was the right to eat the bread which his own hands had earned without leave of anybody.

Lincoln was fond of quoting from the Bible without mentioning the fact, whereas Douglas was often caught differing with the Scriptures. Naturally Lincoln took advantage of his political opponent's lack of Biblical knowledge.

Judge Douglas, in the debate of July 16, 1858, said: "Mr. Lincoln tells you in his speech made in Springfield, 'A house divided against itself cannot stand. I believe this Government cannot endure permanently half slave, half free. I do not expect the Union to be dissolved. I do not expect the house to fall; but I do expect it to cease to be divided. It will become all one thing or all the other.'"

Judge Douglas then proceeded to use as his keynote of his speech Lincoln's sentence: "A house divided against itself cannot stand," arguing eloquently and apparently quite unaware of its Biblical origin.

Referring to Judge Douglas's criticism of his expression, "A house divided against itself cannot stand," Lincoln asked: "Does the judge say it can stand? If he does, then it is a question of veracity not between him and me, but between the judge and an authority of somewhat higher character."

Lincoln's fondness for scriptural stories and incidents is further illustrated when, having appointed a man to a judgeship who had been suspected of having been connected with a certain secret organization which was opposed to Lincoln's renomination, he was remonstrated with and his magnanimity criticized. He replied: "I suppose Judge ———, having been disappointed, did behave badly, but I have scriptural reasons for appointing him. When Moses was on Mount Sinai, getting a commission for Aaron, that same Aaron was at the foot of the mountain making a false god for the people to worship. Yet Aaron got the commission."

As an answer to Douglas's docrine of popular sovereignty Lincoln said that he could not understand why, in the Territories, any man should be "obliged to have a slave if he did not want one. And if any man wants slaves," argued Lincoln, "all other citizens in the Territory have no way of keeping that one man from holding them."

He denounced fiercely the scheme of the Southern slaveholders to annex Cuba as a plan to increase the slave territory. It may be recalled that the conference at Ostend during Buchanan's administration was held for that purpose.

Horace White has published an admirable description of his tour with these debaters. In a parade at Charleston thirty-two young ladies, representing States of the Union, carried banners. This "float" was followed by a handsome young woman on horseback, holding aloft a burgee inscribed: "Kansas, I will be free!" Upon the side of the float was the legend:

Westward the star of empire takes its way;
We girls link on to Lincoln, as our mothers did
   to Clay.

Senator Douglas charged that these debates had been instituted for the purpose of carrying Lincoln into the United States Senate. Although Lincoln denied this, the Democats believed there was some foundation for the assumption.

The meeting at Dayton was a particularly boisterous one. Elijah Parish Lovejoy, a brother of the distinguished Owen Lovejoy, who was very prominent in the abolitionist agitation, had been assassinated there nineteen years before for his anti-slavery opinions, but neither of the speakers referred to the fact.

To show the pro-slavery sentiment that dominated the entire Government at that time, the famous dictum of Chief-Justice Taney in the Dred Scott decision that "a negro had no rights that a white man was bound to respect," may appropriately be recalled.

# II

# Lincoln's Introduction to the East

Abraham Lincoln made his first public appearance in New York at Cooper Union on the night of
the 27th of February, 1860. My anti-slavery attitude
was strengthened by that wonderful speech.

My acquaintance with Abraham Lincoln began
on the afternoon of that memorable day. I was presented to him at his hotel, and I venture to hope
that I made some impression on him. This may
have been due to the fact that at an early age I had
taken an active part in the Republican campaigns,
and had followed with close attention the Lincoln
and Douglas debates as they were reported in the
New York journals. Consequently I could talk intel-
ligently of national politics.

I was on hand early at the Institute that night,
and, having a seat upon the platform, I was able to
observe the manner of the orator as well as to hear
every word he uttered. The way in which he carried himself before the large audience that filled

every nook and corner of that underground hall is engraven on my mind. He was a very homely man. Indeed, he often referred to his homeliness himself. His tall, gaunt body was like a huge clothed skeleton. So large were his feet and so clumsy were his hands that they looked out of proportion to the rest of his figure. No artistic skill could soften his features nor render his appearance less ungainly, but after he began to talk he was awkwardness deified.

In repose, as I saw him on many subsequent occasions, his face seemed dull, but when animated it became radiant with vitalized energy.

No textual report of his Cooper Institute address can possibly give any idea of its great oratorical merits. Mr. Lincoln never ranted, but gave emphatic emphasis to what he wished especially to "put across" by a slowness and marked clearness of enunciation. His voice was unpleasant, almost rasping and shrill at first. Perhaps this was due to the fact that he found it necessary to force it. A little later, he seemed to control his voice better, and his earnestness invited and easily held the attention of his auditors.

To summarize the seven thousand words spoken by Mr. Lincoln on that great occasion would be a difficult task and could not be successfully attempted in these reminiscences. I will only state that his theme was "slavery as the fathers viewed it." Its delivery occupied more than an hour, its entire purpose being to show that the fathers of the Republic merely tolerated slavery where it existed, since interference with it would be resisted by the South; moreover, recognition of the legality of slavery in those States had been the inducement offered to them to enter the Union.

Mr. Lincoln, however, indicated that he was unalterably and inflexibly opposed to the extension of slavery in territory in which it did not exist.

Mr. Lincoln began with a quotation from one of Senator Douglas's speeches, in which the "Little Giant" asserted that the framers of the Constitution understood the slavery question as well as, or better than, their descendants. He brilliantly traced the origin and growth of democracy under the various forms that preceded the final adoption of the Constitution.

As it appeared to an abolitionist in principle, the speaker handled the slavery question somewhat cautiously, chiefly condemning the contemplated repeal of the Missouri Compromise, and opposing the extension of slavery into Territories and States where it did not exist. The appeal that he made to the reason and the common sense of the Southerner was forcible. He denied that the Republicans of the North were sectional, or that they blamed the present generation of the South for the existence of slavery. He went out of his way to condemn the John Brown raid, asserting that the Republican party had no sympathy with that fool-hardy enterprise. He compared the John Brown raid to the previous outbreak at Southampton, Virginia, under the negro, Nat Turner, in which sixty white people, mostly women and children, were destroyed. He denounced the declaration of the Southern people that Northern anti-slavery men had instigated the John Brown incursion at Harper's Ferry, and he showed that the trial of John Brown at Charlestown proved the allegation to be utterly fallacious.

The sentences near the close of Mr. Lincoln's address will serve as the keynote upon which he subsequently based his candidacy for the Presidency in opposition to the extremely radical anti-slavery views of Horace Greeley and William H. Seward.

"Wrong as we think slavery," said Lincoln, "we can afford to let it alone where it is, because that much is due to the necessity arising from its actual presence in the nation; but can we, while our votes will prevent, allow it to spread in the national Territories and to overrun us here in these free States? Let us have faith that right makes might, and in that faith let us dare to do our duty as we understand it."

The reception of these closing words by former Whigs and partially convinced Republicans who were in the audience can hardly be described as enthusiastic. Many of these men left the auditorium that night, as I did, in a seriously thoughtful mood.

Nevertheless, Mr. Lincoln was congratulated by many upon the "boldness" of his views. And, indeed, they seemed radical at a time when nearly every prominent statesman of the country was "trimming" on the slavery question. The great Daniel Webster had ruined his political career some years previously by trying to be "all things to all men" politically.

When I called at Mr. Lincoln's hotel the following morning, I found Mr. Lincoln alone. The shouts of approbation of the previous night were still ringing in my ears, but the figure of the awkward Illinoisan suggested nothing in the way of public enthusiasm or personal distinction. He then and there appeared as a plain, unpretentious man. I ventured to congratulate him upon the success of his speech, and his face brightened. "I am not sure that I made a success," he said, diffidently.

During the remainder of the brief time I was with Mr. Lincoln in his hotel, together with two members of the Republican committee, there was only a general conversation about the Douglas-Lincoln debates, and the intense anti-slavery agitation prevailing in the Kansas and Nebraska Territories and in Illinois.

A few days after that epoch-making speech a prominent Democratic acquaintance, who had often expressed to me in language of bitterness his hatred of all people who opposed the South, assured me that Mr. Lincoln's speech had made him a Free-Soiler, although he had not believed it possible that such a change in his views could ever occur.

In subsequent speeches throughout New England Mr. Lincoln went to greater lengths in his denunciation of slavery. At Hartford, on the 5th of March, he denounced slavery as the enemy of the free working-man; a day later, at New Haven, he characterized slavery as "the snake in the Union bed"; at Norwich, on the ninth of that month, he described Douglas's popular sovereignty as "the sugar-coated slavery pill."

These later speeches greatly strengthened the anti-slavery agitation throughout the North, and went far to settle the opinions of the voters, who were wavering between Douglas's popular sovereignty and the ultra radicalism of Garrison and Phillips.

# III

# How Lincoln Was First Nominated

The Republican National Convention that convened in Chicago, May 16, 1860, proved a complete refutation of the frequently expressed belief that the new party had died with Fremont's defeat in 1856. Some of the ablest and most distinguished men in the country appeared as delegates and as candidates for nomination. During the four years following Fremont's defeat by James Buchanan, of Pennsylvania, former minister to England, the Republican party had been strengthened by the affiliation of many Northern Democrats who were inclined to oppose the extension of slavery. The struggles to exclude the curse of slavery from Kansas and Nebraska had agitated the entire country during these years, and had brought many new voters into the ranks of the Republican party.

William H. Seward was admittedly the great Republican leader and the ablest champion of his party. His speech in the United States Senate on the "Irrepressible Conflict" had made him famous all over the country, and he was constantly talked of by both friends and foes. At least two-thirds of the delegates at the Chicago convention favored his nomination, and even the majority of the delegates from Illinois, Lincoln's own State, while instructed to vote for "Honest Old Abe" as the favorite son, passively favored Seward.

In the New York delegation was Tom Hyer, the noted champion prize-fighter of his generation. He bore the banner of the New York City Republican Club, and was an ardent supporter of Seward. Being a man six feet two and a half inches in height, he presented an imposing figure.

The defeat of Seward's ambition was generally ascribed to an unhealed break between Horace Greeley, Thurlow Weed, and himself. These three men, all eminent in their spheres, constituted what was known then as the "Republican Triumvirate," or what would now be called the "Big Three." This breach occurred in November, 1854, over five years previously. Greeley resented the injustice that he believed had been meted out to him, being sincerely of the opinion that Senator Seward had deceived him, and this unfriendly feeling had fermented into a fully developed hatred.

His letter to Seward announcing "a dissolution of the political firm of Seward, Weed, and Greeley, by the withdrawal of the junior partner," is a part of political history. It is a long epistle, covering more than five pages in Greeley's *Recollections of a Busy Life,* in which is recounted the writer's career in New York, from his start as "a poor young printer" to his affiliations with the political powers of the Empire State. While it contains kindly words for Thurlow Weed, it proclaims the severance of all relations with Seward. In conclusion, it acknowledges acts of kindness by his former partner in politics, and, reiterating that "such acts will be gratefully remembered, the writer takes an eternal farewell."

In the stormy days preceding the Chicago convention the New York *Tribune's* opposition to Seward's nomination had been continuous. But I have always had an idea, based upon a study of the actual occurrences in the convention where I was a looker-on, and from my intimacy with Mr. Greeley, that the factor which had the most to do with Seward's defeat was the fear of Henry S. Lane, Republican candidate for Governor of Indiana, and of Andrew G. Curtin, Republican candidate for Governor of Pennsylvania, that Seward could not carry these two States. This weakness would not only insure defeat of the Presidential ticket, but would carry down with it the aspirations of these two Gubernatorial candidates.

I talked with both of these able politicians on the subject, and the reasons they gave for their opposition to Seward were that he had antagonized the Protestant element of the country and the remnants of the old "Know Nothing party" by his advocacy, in a message to the New York Legislature, of a division of the school funds between Catholic parochial schools and the common or public schools of the States in proportion to the number of Catholics and non-Catholics. How much ground there was for the anxiety of Lane and Curtin I have never been able to settle in my mind. Whether they were unduly alarmed or not, the dissemination of these views among the delegates created a noticeable weakening on the part of Seward's friends.

The battle in the convention was a contest of political giants. Thurlow Weed, to whom Lincoln afterward became greatly attached, was Seward's devoted and loyal friend and champion. He gallantly led the fight for him, ably supported by Edwin D. Morgan, the war Governor of New York, and chairman, at that time, of the National Committee, and also by Henry J. Raymond, the distinguished founder of the New York *Times,* and in later years Lieutenant-Governor of the State of New York.

Before the convention was called to order at

least eight candidates were in the field; to enumer-
ate them:

William H. Seward, of New York.

Abraham Lincoln, of Illinois.

Simon Cameron, of Pennsylvania.

Salmon P. Chase, of Ohio.

Edward Bates, of Missouri.

William L. Dayton, of New Jersey.

Justice John McLean, of the Supreme Court.

Jacob Collamer, of Vermont.

George Ashman, of Massachusetts, was chosen
permanent chairman of the convention, and after
the platform was read Joshua Giddings moved that
it should be amended by inserting a part of the
Declaration of Independence. This was violently
opposed by another delegate in a rather sarcastic
speech, whereupon George William Curtis, one of
the great orators of America, and at the time editor of *Harper's Weekly*, got the floor and in his mel-
lifluous voice said:

"Gentlemen, have you dared to come to this
convention to undo what your fathers did in Independence Hall?"

Curtis's speech carried the amendment.

To impress all wavering delegates, an imposing
political parade through the streets was organized
by Seward's friends. It was great in numbers and
enthusiasm. Hundreds of marchers, among whom

Tom Hyer, in his glossy silk hat, was a prominent figure, were drafted into the parade by the political wire-pullers, but it had no effect in determining the result on the floor of the convention.

Indeed, from my long political experience I have come to the conclusion that these public parades, while imposing for the moment, have no permanent influence upon the voters. The mob of spectators along the streets are there largely as a matter of curiosity, and are not to be swerved from their convictions by any mere spectacle.

While this outside parade was being carried on, Lincoln's friends developed tremendous energy and skill in marshaling the delegates. Among the leaders of the "rail-splitter's" cause were Joseph Medill, the celebrated editor of the Chicago *Tribune*, David Davis, the intimate friend of Lincoln, afterward appointed by him justice of the United States Supreme Court; Norman B. Judd; and Leonard Swett, remarkable for his close resemblance to Lincoln.

Greeley was an intense champion of Edward Bates, who had been a representative from Missouri during the administration of John Quincy Adams.

Greeley's championship of Bates was remarkable for several reasons. Bates was born in Virginia, he had been a lifelong slaveholder, and in politics he was what was known as a "Silver-gray Whig." Consequently he was conservative on the slavery question, clinging to the doctrine of the revolutionary sages that "slavery was an evil to be restricted, not a good to be diffused." Greeley insisted that the position that Bates thus held made him essentially a Republican. While he believed that Bates would poll votes even in the slave States, he was confident that he would rally about him all that was left of the old Whig party.

Greeley, regarding trouble with the Southern States as probably inevitable, yet believed that the nomination of Bates would check and possibly avert an open schism. He did not at the time avow these reasons for supporting Bates, but afterward frankly admitted them. While these views may have influenced his opposition to Seward's nomination, there is no doubt in my mind but that the real reason of his fight against Seward were the grounds hereinbefore stated.

The Free Soil element at Chicago was both prominent and aggressive. A characteristic anecdote is told of Greeley during a caucus at which a Free Soil member shouted, "Let us have a candidate, this time, that represents our advanced convictions against slavery."

"My friend," inquired Greeley, in his falsetto voice, as he rose to his feet, "suppose each Repub-

lican voter in your State were to receive a letter to-
morrow advising him that he (the said voter) had
just lost a brother living in the South, who had left
to him a plantation stocked with slaves. How many
of the two hundred and fifty thousand Republicans would, in response, set free those slaves?"

"I fear I could not stand that test myself," was
the rejoinder.

"Then it is not yet time to nominate an abolitionist," retorted Greeley, sitting down.

This is a good story, but if the incident took
place at all it must have occurred elsewhere than
in the caucus of the New York delegation, for the
reason that Greely, not being a delegate from the
State of New York, could not attend the caucus of
that delegation. He was appointed a delegate from
Oregon, by the special request of the Republicans
of that State, and as such sat in the convention.

Seward had all of the delegates from New York,
Michigan, Massachusetts, and he counted many
followers in other States.

Lincoln had a strong following from his own
State, and on the first ballot mustered one hundred and two votes out of a total of four hundred
and sixty-six. Seward received one hundred and
seventy-two and a half on the second ballot; then
Cameron turned his votes over to Lincoln, and
thirteen of the Bates delegates followed suit. On

the third ballot Lincoln's vote had increased to two hundred and thirty-one and a half, while Seward's was only one hundred and eighty. When the break started I turned to my neighbor in the gallery and remarked, "Seward is defeated; Lincoln will be nominated."

"No," he objected; "this is only one delegation, and Seward's friends are too devotedly attached to his fortunes. They will never go over to his opponent."

"And what will Greeley do?" I asked.

"Greeley will be left with only his hatred," he rejoined.

And yet, even as we were speaking, the tide had turned. Delegate after delegate came over to Lincoln, and the final ballot gave him three hundred and fifty-four votes and the nomination. When the result was announced there was an outbreak from the galleries which had been packed with Lincoln sympathizers, but the New York delegates sat silent and sullen in their seats. It seemed a long time, although it was really only a few minutes, before William M. Evarts, the distinguished member of the New York bar, who later became Secretary of State under President Hayes, and Senator from the State of New York, rose and moved, presumably with Seward's acquiescence, that Lincoln's nomination be made unanimous. Then the applause broke out again and this time it was much more general and spontaneous.

Hannibal Hamlin, of Maine, was nominated for Vice-President practically without opposition. The singular coincidence that the last syllable of Lincoln's first name, "Abraham," and the first syllable of his last name, "Lincoln," form the name "Hamlin," attracted wide attention at that time.

A great many anti-slavery advocates in the North differed with Lincoln as regards his views on the grave question of the immediate extinction of slavery in the Southern States. They did not understand him.

They did not comprehend that he was at heart thoroughly imbued with the unrighteousness of property in human beings, but that he felt it was good policy to go gradually, step by step, hoping to unite the entire North and so bring about the ultimate abolishment of slavery; whereas, if the policy for the immediate extinction of slavery should be adopted it must inevitably have disrupted the Republican party.

I was present at that convention, not as a delegate, but as a "looker-on" and a student of American politics. I need not say that I learned much about the finesse and spirit of compromise that enters into all national conventions.

From a brief conversation which I had with Mr. Greeley, I understood that while he disclaimed having effected Seward's defeat, he was only moderately gratified at Lincoln's nomination.

In his well-known volume of *Recollections* he intimates that he exerted much less influence in bringing about Seward's defeat than I gathered from the conversation I had with him on the morning following Lincoln's nomination.

The demand of the people of the North, where the Republican strength lay exclusively, was for a candidate who would appeal to both Free-Soilers and abolitionists. Between these factions there was an almost impassable gulf.

Now as the years have rolled on Lincoln has grown steadily in the love and admiration of the American people, and the unjust criticism which was made by the abolitionists at the time of his nomination, namely, that he did not favor the abolition of slavery in the States because he was born in the South, is regarded with disdain. The abolitionists in their intemperate criticism used language, in discussing Lincoln, hardly less acrimonious than that employed by the "fire-eaters" of the South; but they had no recourse except to vote for him. Thus were added thousands of unwilling votes to swell the Lincoln aggregate in the November election.

The Democratic convention had convened at an earlier date in Charleston, South Carolina, the city of my birth. After quarreling over a platform for a week, the convention was split by the withdrawal of the majority of the delegates of the slave States, following the adoption of the plank favoring the Douglas "popular sovereignty" doctrine.

After fifty-seven ballots for President, in which Douglas had the majority in every instance, but not the two-thirds required for nomination in Democratic conventions, the convention adjourned on May 3, 1860, to reassemble at Baltimore, June 18. There, the places of the seceders having been filled, Douglas received one hundred and seventy-three and a half votes on the first ballot and one hundred and eighty-one and a half on the second, still lacking the vote of two-thirds of the three hundred and three delegates in convention. On motion of Sanford E. Church, of New York, who, in later years, became chief-justice of the Court of Appeals of that State, he was declared the nominee. Herschel V. Johnson, of Georgia, was named as candidate for Vice-President.

The remnant of the Charleston convention gathered itself together in a separate convention, also held in Baltimore, on the eleventh day of June. It adjourned on the 25th of that month, when John C. Breckenridge, of Kentucky,—at that time Vice-President under Buchanan—was unanimously named for President, with Gen. Joseph H. Lane, of Oregon, as his running mate.

In the Charleston convention Benjamin F. Butler, of Massachusetts, who during the Civil War became identified with the North and was made a major-general in the Union Army, cast a solitary vote for Jefferson Davis as the Democratic candidate for President.

The three-cornered contest that followed between Lincoln, Douglas, and Breckenridge is paralleled in American political history by the famous campaign of 1824 when Jackson, Adams, Clay, and Crawford, all of the same party, were running for the Presidency. As none of the latter received a majority of the electoral vote, the election, under the provisions of the Constitution, was thrown into the House of Representatives, where John Quincy Adams received the nomination.

When the committee went to Springfield to notify Mr. Lincoln of his nomination, Judge Kelly, of Pennsylvania, known, because of his service of over thirty years in Congress, as the father of the House of Representatives, was one of the committee. The judge was unusually large in stature, and his great height attracted Mr. Lincoln, who, upon shaking hands with him, asked, "What is your height, Judge?"

"About six feet three," said Judge Kelly. "What is yours, Mr. Lincoln."

"Six feet four," replied Lincoln, with a smile, pulling himself up to his full stature.

"Pennsylvania," said Judge Kelly, "bows to Illinois. My dear man, for years my heart has been aching for a President that I could 'look up to,' and I have found him in the land where we thought there was none but 'Little Giants.'"

Lincoln replied, "There is one man in this country who, though little in stature, is a giant in mind, and he has given me much hard work to do."

Mr. Lincoln's reply to the committee that visited Springfield on May 19, to notify him of his nomination, and his formal letter of acceptance, dated May 23, avoided all reference to what Mr. Seward had described as "the impending crisis." In his letter Mr. Lincoln pledged "due regard to the rights of all States and Territories and people of the nation, to the inviolability of the Constitution, and the perpetual union, harmony, and prosperity of all." This assurance satisfied neither slaveholders of the South nor anti-slave men of the North. This letter often rose to haunt Lincoln in the latter part of the war, after he had issued the Emancipation Proclamation which gave freedom to all the slaves.

Mr. Lincoln was in the office of the Springfield *Journal* when he received the first notification of his nomination. After allowing the assembled people to congratulate him, he said, "There is a little woman down at our house that would like to hear the news," and he started at once for home.

# IV

# How Lincoln Was First Elected

Not long after his nomination I went to Chicago and thence to Springfield. When I called at the modest Lincoln home, in order to offer my congratulations, I found him eager to obtain every ray of light upon the prospects of the coming campaign.

"What are the chances of my election?" he asked, as he took my hand.

"You are going to get the entire North," I replied, "on account of the Democratic division between Breckenridge and Douglas."

"That is my own way of calculating," he assented, "but I am glad to get the views of everybody of experience in political matters."

"Mr. Dittenhoefer is absolutely correct in his figuring," put in a bystander, and the glimmer of a smile of satisfaction passed over Mr. Lincoln's rugged countenance. I stepped back and stood looking and wondering. Typically Western he seemed to be in face, figure, and dress. How would he bear himself if called upon to direct the destinies of the Republic? Let me say frankly that, at this early day, no suspicion of his real greatness had ever entered my mind. I knew he was an able man, and I was content to hope that he might be strong enough to cope with the coming crisis in national affairs.

The Republican campaign, which began in earnest by the middle of June and lasted until the night before election day in November, differed in many respects from any other in my recollection.

I believe that there was more sincerity of soul put into the efforts to win by fair means than has appeared in more recent national contests.

A few days before the election of 1860 I made a speech at Cooper Institute, which began as follows:

> "With banners waving and with bugle horns,
> We are coming, Father Abraham, five hundred
>     thousand strong,
> One blast upon the bugle horn is worth a
>     thousand men."

This was repeated by numerous speakers on the stump throughout the country.

Memories of these parades, stump speeches, and bonfires linger with me vividly. The marching clubs were called "Wide Awakes," and upon the oil-cloth cloaks, cut amply long in order to protect their wearers from the weather, the words "Wide Awake," in tall, white letters, were painted. Each man carried a swinging torch which maintained an upright position no matter how it was held. The campaign developed numerous parades of these "Wide Awakes" in cities and towns throughout the country.

The Republican National Committee was not in possession of large funds, and each organization financed itself. It is doubtful if the National Committee had more than $100,000 to spend, and most of this went for printing and postage. There was no "yellow-dog fund" in those days. Had it been necessary for Mr. Lincoln or his managers to raise a half-million dollars, or go down to defeat, Lincoln would have lost out.

Our "infant industries" had not yet been developed and "brought to a head by the poultice of protection." The late Senator Hanna would have regarded the prospects of a successful campaign without contribution from the protected interests as exceedingly doubtful.

I threw all my energy into this campaign, and, though young, I was frequently making several speeches during a day and evening. I marched with the "Wide Awakes," and was sent to different parts of the State, where, with other speakers, I addressed large audiences. The temper of my hearers was not always encouraging.

I have always doubted whether Seward's partisan adherents in central New York gave really loyal support to Lincoln, since it continued to rankle in their breasts that the sentiment of two-thirds of the convention, originally in favor of Seward, had been turned to Lincoln through the machinations of Horace Greeley, Reuben E. Fenton—afterward Governor of the State of New York—and other prominent anti-Seward men.

No attempt was made by the Republicans to campaign in the Southern States, where the breach existing between the Douglas and Brecken-ridge adherents was remorselessly unrelenting. The drift in those States was naturally unani-mously in favor of Breckenridge, and it was early recognized that Douglas, though a Democrat, would not carry a single Southern State.

In the North the contest lay between Lincoln and Douglas. Breckenridge and Bell counted com-paratively few and scattered followers, and their names awakened no enthusiasm.

Stephen A. Douglas was one of the best types of

the American aggressive politician this country ever produced. I heard Douglas speak on several occasions. His figure was short and chunky, hardly measuring up to his popular title of the "Little Giant." He was very eloquent, but his campaign theme, "Popular Sovereignty," was never a drawing-card in the North, and the practical application of this doctrine was really restricted to the Territories, including "Bleeding Kansas." The many speeches that Douglas made throughout the North only had the effect of consolidating the opponents of "Squatter Sovereignty."

The adoption by Southern States of the principle of "State rights," which in effect was only another name for the right of secession, was the reason advanced to justify the rebellion which broke out with such fury in the later years; but the demand for the right to introduce slavery into new territory was, in my opinion, the impelling reason that finally made the Civil War inevitable.

In the free States the division of the popular vote was chiefly between Lincoln and Douglas, while the slave States were largely for Breckenridge, with a minority for Bell, the "Silver-gray Whig" candidate.

The totals in the two sections are interesting as matters of record:

|              | *Lincoln* | *Douglas* | *Breckenridge* | *Bell* |
|--------------|-----------|-----------|----------------|--------|
| Free States  | 1,831,180 | 1,128,049 | 279,211        | 130,151 |
| Slave States | 26,430    | 163,574   | 570,871        | 515,973 |
| Total        | 1,857,610 | 1,291,623 | 850,082        | 646,124 |

Mr. Lincoln had 180 electoral votes to 123 for all the other candidates. Every free State, with the exception of New Jersey, went for him, and even New Jersey gave him four votes, the three remaining going to the "Little Giant." Breckenridge, with a much smaller popular vote than Douglas, had 72 electoral votes, while Douglas, with a larger popular vote, had only 12 in all.

As Mr. Greeley accurately summed it up: "A united North succeeded over a divided South; while in 1856 a united South triumphed over a divided North."

Let us remember that a majority of the members of the Supreme Court had shown strong Southern proclivities; the Senate was also largely anti-Republican, and the House of Representatives had a very mixed political complexion, owing to the fact that many of its members had been chosen in the October election preceding the Presidential election.

Such was as the national situation after the popular verdict had been declared in favor of Lincoln and Hamlin. The South could not reconcile itself to the result. Trouble was in the air, but the North did not yet realize the inevitability of civil war.

It was a long, anxious winter for the President-elect, and the strain upon him then was even more noticeable than after he assumed the burden of his great office.

He delivered his pathetic farewell address to his neighbors and friends in Springfield on February 11, 1861, and the following extract is entitled to a place in this record:

> My friends: No one, not in my situation, can appreciate my feeling of sadness at this parting. To this place, and the kindness of these people, I owe everything. Here I have lived a quarter of a century, and have passed from a young to an old man. Here my children have been born, and here one is buried. I now leave, not knowing when or whether I ever may return, with a task before me greater than that which rested upon Washington. Without the assistance of that Divine Being who ever attended him I cannot succeed. With that assistance I cannot fail. Trusting in Him who can go with me, and yet remain with you and be everywhere for good, let us confidently hope that all will yet be well. To His care commending you, as I hope in your prayers you will commend me, I bid you an affectionate farewell.

Many of Mr. Lincoln's neighbors were in tears. I was not at Springfield on that day, but I heard directly from men who were present that the pain of separation was keenly felt by all classes of society.

Mr. Lincoln left Springfield not to return.

## V
# The Journey to the Capital

The trip from Springfield to Washington was one of continuous enthusiasm, the President-elect receiving an ovation at every city en route. The first halt was made at Indianapolis, where he addressed a meeting, at which the famous War-Governor Morton presided. On this occasion he declared that "the preservation of the Union rests entirely with the people."

On the same day he spoke before a joint meeting of the Indiana Legislature, choosing for his theme: "The Union, is it a marriage bond or a free-love arrangement?"

When about to cross the Ohio River into Virginia, a slave State, he gave it as his opinion that devotion to the Constitution was equally great on both sides of the stream, and he went on to emphasize the right of the majority to rule.

Arriving at Cleveland, he made an address in which he referred to the apprehended trouble as "altogether artificial, due only to differences in political opinion." "Nothing," he declared, "is going to hurt the South; they are citizens of this common country and we have no power to change their conditions. What, then, is the matter with them? Why all these complaints? Doesn't this show how artificial is the crisis? It has no foundation in fact. It can't be argued up and it can't be argued down. Let it alone, and it will go down of itself."

This would seem to show that Mr. Lincoln really believed that the trouble in the South would blow over. How sadly he was mistaken! It was not until he arrived in the East and learned from trustworthy sources of the danger confronting him between New York and Washington that he accepted the situation as it actually existed.

Buffalo was the next stopping-place, and the mayor and a large assemblage welcomed the President-elect. The stability of the Union was the speaker's theme, but he reiterated that he relied more upon divine assistance than help from human hands and hearts.

At Albany Governor Morgan presided over a public meeting, at which Lincoln again declared that he would be "President not of a party, but of a nation." Later in the day he delivered another address, in which he said that "the mightiest of tasks confronted the humblest of Presidents."

He remained two days in New York City, where he delivered two addresses. To a large audience, over which the unsympathetic Democratic mayor, Fernando Wood, presided, Mr. Lincoln expressed his doubts as to the situation in quaint language. He likened the Union to a ship and its traditions to the cargo, saying that he was willing and anxious to save both the ship and cargo, but if not both, the cargo would have to go overboard for the safety of the ship.

I heard that address and it gave me the impression that Mr. Lincoln had become bolder in the expression of his feeling against the continuance of slavery in the South. To-day it recalls itself to me as being the first gleam of emancipation.

The speaker was more grave and serious than usual; his voice was harsh and his manner indicated either fatigue or anxiety regarding the future. I detected a decided change in Mr. Lincoln since seeing him at Springfield; he was a man carrying a burden that grew heavier day by day.

The journey toward Washington was resumed on February 21, a halt being made at Trenton for the President-elect to address, separately, the Senate and the Assembly of New Jersey.

Later in the afternoon the train reached Philadelphia, where a reception presided over by the mayor was tendered to him. In consequence of reports of danger he was practically smuggled away from Philadelphia, being hurried in a closed carriage to the old Prince Street station, on South Broad Street, where an engine and one car was waiting. This was run through to Baltimore and thence over the Baltimore and Ohio branch to Washington.

A large number of citizens in Baltimore, not confined by any means to the mob, were bitterly hostile to "the Yankee President," as they derisively described the man from Illinois. That the precautions taken were justified was proven within two months by the murderous assault upon the Sixth Massachusetts regiment during its march through Baltimore.

A little over four years later, when Lincoln's funeral cortège passed through Baltimore, a complete change of feeling had taken place. In the selfsame city which had been considered unsafe for President Lincoln to pass through, the first great demonstration of grief occurred.

The President-elect arrived in Washington on February 27, and although no outward evidence of the coming storm was observable, there was an intense feeling of anxiety among all classes at the national capital; it must be remembered that most of the office-holders were Southerners and that the city was filled with residents sympathetic with the South. In a reply to the serenade at his hotel on the evening of February 28, Mr. Lincoln lamented the misunderstanding that existed between the people of the North and the South, and reiterated his determination to enforce equal rights under the Constitution to all citizens. He pledged an impartial administration of the law.

I was present at the delivery of Lincoln's inaugural address, a wonderful piece of English composition which will continue to live when the monuments of bronze and marble erected to his memory have crumbled to dust. In it occur these unforgetable words:

> With malice toward none, with charity for all, with firmness in the right, as God gives us to see the right, let us strive to finish the work we are in; to bind up the nation's wounds; to care for him who shall have borne the battle, and for his widow and orphan—to do all which may achieve and cherish a just and lasting peace among ourselves, and with all nations.

The President impressed me as being very serious in manner. His voice sounded shrill, but he was talking at high pitch in order that he might be heard by as many as possible of the immense crowd. The assemblage was orderly, respectful, and attentive. Little by little his auditors warmed toward him, until finally the applause became overwhelming, spontaneous, and enthusiastic. Then, for the first time, it dawned upon me that

Lincoln was not only the strong man needed at this crisis of our national affairs, but one of the few great men of all time; and I may say safely that this conviction was shared by all within hearing of his voice.

Thirty-nine days later the cannon were booming at Fort Moultrie and Fort Sumter.

# VI

# Stories and Incidents

Apparently the world is never weary of asking what was the true Abraham Lincoln, and every side-light upon his character is significant.

A man whom I knew well discovered the President at his office counting greenbacks and inclosing them in an envelope. He asked Mr. Lincoln how he could spare the time for such a task in the midst of the important duties that were pressing upon him.

Lincoln replied: "The President of the United States has a multiplicity of duties not specified in the Constitution of the laws. This is one of them. It is money which belongs to a negro porter from the Treasury Department. He is now in the hospital, too sick to sign his name, and according to his wish I am putting a part of it aside in an envelope, properly labeled, to save it for him."

An eye-witness relates that one day while walking along a shaded path from the Executive Mansion to the War Office, he saw the tall form of the President seated on the grass. He afterward learned that a wounded soldier, while on his way to the White House seeking back pay and a pension, had met the President and had asked his assistance. Whereupon Mr. Lincoln sat down, looked over the soldier's papers, and advised him what to do; he ended by giving him a note directing him to the proper place to secure attention.

Driving up to a hospital one day he saw one of the patients walking directly in the path of his team. The horses were checked none too soon; then Mr. Lincoln saw that he was nothing but a boy and had been wounded in both eyes. He got out of the carriage and questioned the poor fellow, asking him his name, his service, and his residence. "I am Abraham Lincoln," he said, upon leaving; and the sightless face lighted at the President's words of sympathy. The following day the chief of the hospital delivered to the boy a commission in the Army of the United States as first lieutenant. The papers bore the President's signature and were accompanied by an order retiring him on three-quarters pay for the years of helplessness that lay before him.

"Some of my generals complain that I impair discipline in the Army by my pardons and respites," Lincoln once said. "But it rests me, after a hard day's work, if I can find some excuse for saving a man's life, and I go to bed happy as I think how joyous the signing of my name will make him and his family and his friends."

I once heard Mr. Lincoln telling a number of Congressmen in the anteroom of the White House that in the distribution of patronage care should be taken of the disabled soldiers and the widows and orphans of deceased soldiers, and these views were subsequently conveyed to the Senate in a message which contained the following language:

Yesterday a little endorsement of mine went to you in two cases of postmasterships sought for widows whose husbands have fallen in the battles of the war. These cases occurring on the same day brought me to reflect more attentively than I had before as to what is fairly due in the dispensing of patronage to the men who, by fighting our battles, bear the chief burden of saving our country. My conclusion is that, other claims and qualifications being equal, they have the better right; and this is especially applicable to the disabled soldier and the deceased soldier's family.

It may not be out of place to consider here what would be Mr. Lincoln's attitude toward the irrepressible conflict that has been raging with such fierceness all over the world, between capital and labor, and which is ever increasing in intensity. I quote the following extracts from Lincoln's message to Congress as showing his views on that question:

It is not needed, not fitting here, that a general argument should be made in favor of popular institutions, but there is one point not so hackneyed to which I ask a brief attention—it is an effort to place capital on an equal footing with, if not above, labor in the structure of the Government. Capital is the fruit of labor, and could never have existed if labor had not existed. Labor is the superior of capital, and deserves much higher consideration.

It will thus be seen that the President's sympathies were with struggling labor, and against the powerful capitalists, and that he would exercise his constitutional powers to promote the welfare of the laboring class. That attitude is in keeping with the broad humanitarian principles that always influenced Mr. Lincoln's actions.

Truly, Lincoln's great, tender heart was always open to the sufferings of humanity; certainly his sympathy was never branded by the limitations of creed or dogma. He never became a member of any church, but no one could doubt that he was a man of deep religious feeling. I remember on one occasion hearing him say, "Religion is a matter of faith; all good men will be saved." Judging by our standard of to-day, this utterance would class him with the Unitarians.

Upon one occasion, after he had become our President, he visited the Five Points Mission in New York, at that time a notorious slum, and addressed a number of children; while there he gave no intimation that he was President of the United States. When he was leaving the teacher thanked him, and asked who he was. He simply answered, "Abraham Lincoln, of Illinois."

I have spoken of seeing Lincoln smile, but I never remember hearing him laugh heartily, even when he was convulsing every one about him with one of inimitably told stories. And yet he apparently enjoyed exciting the mirth of others, and to that extent, at least, he seemed to enter into the spirit of the comedy. Many of the great humorists of the world have been men of melancholy mood, and both tears and laughter are based on the same precious essence.

I was often in Washington in those days, and I recollect frequently seeing the great President walking on Pennsylvania Avenue, with "Little Tad" clasping his hand. The fact that he took Tad with him on his important mission to Richmond, where he attended the conference with some of the leaders of the Confederacy, shows the companionship and intense affection between the President and the son of his old age.

Once while Mrs. Lincoln was at Manchester, Vermont, she received a message from the President, saying, "All is well, including Tad's pony and the goats." A little later he asked her to tell "dear Tad that poor nanny-goat is lost."

I often saw the President sitting in the White House in carpet slippers, and wearing an old bombazine coat out at the elbows. Indeed, Mr. Lincoln was not created to adorn fashionable society, and did not care for it. Clothing never troubled him, while Mrs. Lincoln set much store upon appearances and was concerned over her husband's indifference to them.

The severe trials which confronted him, greater than any other President encountered, and the heavy burden that rested on him, did not blunt his finer feelings.

In a conversation with Mr. Lincoln, in which his visit to Richmond came up, I casually inquired what he thought should be done with Jefferson Davis at the end of the war, which appeared then to be approaching. After a moment's deliberation his sad face brightened as he answered that, if he had his way, he would let him die in peace on his Southern plantation. I remember well that at that time my interpretation of his words was that he would not permit any punishment to be inflicted on Jefferson Davis, unless it were absolutely demanded by the American people.

During the early part of President Johnson's administration, after the collapse of the rebellion, Davis was captured and brought on habeas corpus proceedings before a Virginia court and released on bail. Horace Greeley, Gerritt Smith, and other Northern anti-slavery men became sureties on the bail bond, but no proceedings were ever taken to bring Davis to trial. He was allowed to die in peace on his Southern plantation.

Can history show any thought more magnanimous in the life of a ruler or statesman than this? Lincoln urged Meade, after the battle of Gettysburg to pursue Lee in retreat and with one bold stroke end the war. The order was peremptory, but a friendly note was attached, as follows:

The order I enclose is not of record. If you succeed, you need not publish the order. If you fail, publish it. Then, if you succeed, you will have all the credit of the movement. If not, I'll take care of the responsibility.

A striking example of the President's unselfish refusal to use his official position for the advancement of any member of his family, is found in his letter to General Grant, asking for a commission for his son, Robert.

Please read and answer this letter as though I was not President, but only a friend. My son, now in his twenty-second year, having graduated at Harvard, wishes to see something of the war before it ends. I do not wish to put him in the ranks, nor yet give him a commission to which those who have already served long are better entitled and better qualified to hold.

Could he, without embarrassment to you or detriment to the service, go into your military family with some nominal rank; I, and not the public, furnishing his necessary means? If not, say so without the least hesitation, because I am as anxious and as deeply interested that you shall not be encumbered as you can be yourself.

Mr. Lincoln was famous for disposing of office-seekers without leaving a sting behind. H. C. Whitney told this story to a friend of mine:

"I had business in Washington in 1861 pertaining to the Indian service, and I remarked to Mr. Lincoln that, 'Everything is drifting into the war, and I guess you will have to put me in the Army.' Lincoln smiled and said: 'I'm making generals now. In a few days I'll be making quartermasters, then I'll see to you.'"

Lincoln, referring to the criticisms made upon the administration, particularly in regard to matters entirely outside of its jurisdiction, said that he was reminded of a certain Long Island fisherman who was accustomed to go out eeling every morning. In the old days, he asserted, he never caught less than a pailful of eels, but since this administration came into power he had to be content with half a pailful. Therefore he was going to vote for the Democratic party; he *wanted a change.*

# VII

# Four Years of Stress and Strain

Buchanan belonged to the school of American pro-slavery Presidents. During the last year of his administration he was as completely dominated by the Southern members of his Cabinet as were the Merovingian kings by their mayors of the palace. By blackest treachery, John B. Floyd, Secretary of War, and Isaac Toucey, Secretary of the Navy, gorged the armories and navy-yards located in the slave States with arms, ordnance, and all manner of munitions of war, thus anticipating months ahead what the Southern politicians regarded as the "inevitable conflict." The Federal Government, with the spineless Buchanan at its head, was utterly unprepared for the crisis.

Such was the situation when President Lincoln took the oath of office; such the already divided nation when the irresolute, truckling Buchanan handed over the destinies of the Republic to his successor.

No heavier burden ever was imposed upon a ruler of any people.

Mr. Lincoln was only partially fortunate in choosing his Cabinet. Seward was inevitable. Chase was a lucky guess, because he was without a record as a financier. Cameron was a mistake, and the error was not rectified as promptly as it should have been. The other members, with the possible exception of Gideon Welles, who received the Navy portfolio, were negligible.

The administration found itself without an army, many of its ablest officers having left the service to take up arms against the Federal Government. The rank and file of the army was fairly loyal, but the troops had been so scattered by Buchanan's secretary of war that they could not be mobilized promptly when the hour of danger came. Despite the plottings of Secretary Toucey, however, the vessels of the Navy were so dispersed that the Confederacy was unable to seize many of them. This was most fortunate, since it made possible the prompt establishment of a Federal blockade over important Atlantic and Gulf ports.

Legal business took me to Washington about four months after Lincoln's first inauguration and I called at the White House, in company with Mr. Fenton. Although a score of men were present in the different parts of the large room overlooking the South lot, Mr. Lincoln was walking the floor in a preoccupied manner, evidently deeply distressed.

The Federal troops had just been defeated at Big Bethel by a much smaller force under Magruder, a crushing blow for the Union arms.

I suggested to Mr. Fenton that we should retire, as the visit seemed inopportune, but the President's grave face showed signs of recognition when he saw Mr. Fenton. He stopped, and as we approached him, he said:

"The storm is upon us; it will be much worse before it is better. I suppose there was a divine purpose in thrusting this terrible responsibility upon me, and I can only hope for more than human guidance. I am only a mortal in the hands of destiny. I am ready for the trial and shall do my best, because I know I am acting for the right."

He did not mention the defeat that had occurred only two days before, but it was evident that he comprehended fully the desperate situation that confronted the Federal Government.

Big Bethel was within ten miles of Fortress Monroe, and I subsequently learned from a member of the Cabinet that the utmost anxiety existed regarding the safety of that post. If treachery existed among its officers, the secret has been kept until this day, but one can understand the agonizing suspense of that hour. Had the great fortress at Old Point Comfort fallen into the hands of the Confederacy, the early part of the war would necessarily have been fought upon entirely different lines.

Mr. Lincoln possessed no knowledge of the art of war, but he had sufficient intuitive foresight to comprehend what the loss of control of the entrance to Chesapeake Bay and the mouth of the James River would mean. Although he said so little, this meeting and the few words he used were most impressive, and are stamped deep upon my memory.

As I have just remarked, military and naval technicalities did not matter much to Lincoln, and he was accustomed to brush them aside in his familiar, humorous way. When Mr. Bushnell brought to Washington the plans for the *Monitor,* the recent invention of Mr. Ericsson, which became famous in the sea-fight with the rebel *Merrimac,* most of the naval officers expressed doubts as to the efficiency of the *Monitor* in a naval fight. Mr. Lincoln's opinion was asked. He said he knew little about ships, but he "did understand a flatboat, and this invention was flat enough."

Later, at a meeting of the Army board, when asked by Admiral Smith what he thought of the *Monitor,* he remarked, with his most quizzical look,

"Well, I feel a good deal about it as a fat girl did when she put her foot in her stocking; she thought there was something in it."

All present laughed at this drollery, but it was the way Lincoln sometimes took of conveying a really serious thought.

At that period of the war and until the battle of Gettysburg, two years later, Southern leaders acted upon the theory that the people of the North were greatly divided in their sympathies, and that the "Copperheads" would either develop sufficient strength to stop the war; or, in the event of invasion of the Northern States, they would take up arms in support of the Confederacy. John Morgan's raid into Ohio encouraged that belief, although he was captured and imprisoned; but the utter indifference shown by the Pennsylvania "Copperheads," who had talked loudest in favor of the Southern cause, completely disillusioned the Confederate chiefs. Vallandigham and Voorhees were shown to be without great influence. I had a direct statement from a member of the Lincoln Cabinet that the President did not approve of Vallandigham's arrest by General Burnside, or his trial by court-martial and banishment to the Southern lines. Lincoln declared the proceedings to be those of an over-zealous general.

Defeat after defeat of the Northern forces followed that of Big Bethel. The raw volunteers from the Northern States could not successfully oppose the better-trained Southern troops, led by West Point graduates.

Mr. Lincoln never lost heart; his courage never abated during those terrible months, while many men close to him were in a mental condition of dismay and panic.

The day of Burnside's defeat at Fredericksburg Lincoln spent hours in the office of the War Department in dressing-gown and slippers, forgetting even to eat. When he heard of the great disaster he bowed his head in despair, and murmured, "If there is any man out of perdition who suffers more than I do, I pity him."

Sufficient credit was never given to Thurlow Weed for his successful efforts in England to prevent recognition of the Confederacy. Mr. Lincoln described Weed as "a master of masters in politics," and sent him on that difficult mission late in 1861 when the situation looked very dark. Our able minister at the court of St. James's, Charles Francis Adams, possessed Mr. Lincoln's entire confidence, but the President deemed it advisable to have a special commissioner to present his protest against the apprehended British recognition of the Southern Confederacy.

The day before Mr. Weed's departure I met him

in the rotunda of the old Astor House, and found him imbued with more hope than I felt, regarding the conflict with the South. Of course, he made no mention of his intended mission to England, thinking that he could get away without the fact becoming known. He was disappointed, however, as the day following his departure all the newspapers published the news of his special embassy. There were no Atlantic cables in those days, and by prompt action on his arrival he managed to hold his first interview with Lord Russell before official information reached the British Cabinet from Washington regarding the purpose of his presence in London.

Henry Ward Beecher also visited England at Mr. Lincoln's request, possibly at the suggestion of John Bright, who was almost the only prominent Briton who remained friendly to the Federal cause. Gladstone, Palmerston, and Disraeli were at that time in open sympathy with the Confederacy.

Mr. Beecher's mission was wholly unofficial, and his efforts were devoted to delivering addresses, such as only he could make, throughout England. These speeches and Mr. Weed's efforts created such a wave of popular sentiment in behalf of the Federal cause that the British Cabinet, if ever it had the purpose, was deterred from recognizing the States in rebellion. It was the same kind of moral suasion employed by Gladstone prior to the Russo-Turkish War of 1877–78, and which prevented England from going to the defense of Turkey, then her ally.

The relief experienced through General Lee's defeat at Gettysburg and his retreat across Maryland into Virginia was followed, ten days later (July, 1863), by the draft riots in New York.

The horrors of those three days have never been fully described.

Led and encouraged by Southern sympathizers, who had retained the feelings they held before the war, the rabble of the city surged through the streets, destroying property, burning a negro orphan-asylum, and killing black men. Nominally a protest against enforced enlistment, the riots were really an uprising of the dangerous element that existed in the city at the time.

I lived in Thirty-fourth Street, near Eighth Avenue, and had been a persistent speaker against the extension of slavery and in favor of the Federal cause. The day before the riots began, an anonymous note was received by my family, stating that our home would be attacked and that we had best leave the city. We did not heed the warning.

On the first day of the riots, July 13, 1863, a crowd gathered in front of my house, shouting: "Down with the abolitionists!" "Death to Dittenhoefer!" I sent a messenger for the police, and a squad arrived as the leaders of the mob were preparing to break in my door. Active club work dispersed the crowd, and by order of the captain of the precinct several policemen were kept on guard until the end of the riots.

It was at this time that I met Mrs. Carson, the daughter of the only Union man in South Carolina, who, with her father, was compelled, after the firing on Fort Sumter, to leave South Carolina, while his property was confiscated. I had been anxious to sell my house in Thirty-fourth Street. Noticing a "For Sale" sign on the property, Mrs. Carson called on me and expressed a willingness to buy the house at the price named, asking me to see Samuel Blatchford, who in later years became a Supreme Court Judge of the United States, and who, she said, was the head of an association raising funds for her support in New York. I saw Judge Blatchford, and a contract was signed for the sale. Later, in consequence of the serious illness of my wife, I was obliged to ask Judge Blatchford to cancel the contract, saying that, by way of making up for the disappointment, I would gladly contribute a sum of money to the fund for Mrs. Carson. The contract was accordingly canceled. I never saw Mrs. Carson afterward. About a year before the close of the rebellion, Mr. Lincoln offered to appoint me judge of the district court of South Carolina, my native State, but my increasing business in the city of New York and the disinclination of my wife to move to South Carolina compelled me to decline the honor.

A little while before the offer of the Carolina judgeship was made me by the President I received a letter signed by Mrs. Carson, in which the writer said that the President had asked her to recommend a man for the position, and, remembering what I had done years before, she had suggested my name to him. For a long time I could not think who Mrs. Carson could be, until my wife reminded me of the incident of the sale of the house.

Patriotic  neglect of self-interest in behalf of the salvation of the Union caused thousands of Northerners to lose opportunities for accumulating wealth from the vast sums of money disbursed by the Government; but there was a class at home and in Congress that neglected no chance to enrich itself. Its leaders were more concerned about the commercial phase of the conflict than the triumph of the Federal arms.

They gambled on the destiny of the Republic, and their sources of information reached to the innermost sanctuaries of Government departments.

On advance information of a staggering defeat

to the Northern arms, they bought gold for a rise. Early news of a Federal victory caused them to sell the precious metal for a decline. This transaction was described by these gamblers in the nation's life-blood as "coppering old Lincoln."

This detestable clan pushed its representatives into the very councils of state, asserting its right to dictate the policy of the country, foreign and domestic. Its members were as intolerably arrogant as if they had amassed their wealth by the strictest integrity.

During a great part of the war President Lincoln, unsuspected by him, was surrounded by a coterie of professional heroes, commercial grafters, and alleged statesmen, every one of whom was in politics for personal profit. Many "shining lights" then lauded for their patriotism have long since been exposed as selfish and corrupt egotists. Close as some of these unworthy persons contrived to get to Mr. Lincoln, they were never able to besmirch him in any way.

During one of my visits to the White House some weeks before the promulgation of the Emancipation Proclamation, I had the temerity to refer to the oft-reported plan of Mr. Lincoln, before the rebellion burst upon the country, to free the Southern slaves by purchase. It was a theme that had often engaged my thoughts. After the beginning of the war and a realization that the conflict was costing more than $1,000,000 per day, I had become somewhat reconciled to the idea.

Mr. Lincoln was slow to answer, saying, in effect, that however wise the idea might have been, it was too late to revive it. He did not intimate that he had in contemplation the Emancipation Proclamation which was to take effect January 1, 1863.

Mr. Lincoln had all the figures about slave property at his finger-ends, but, much to my regret, I did not make a memorandum of the interview and, therefore, cannot recall the exact number of slaves that he estimated would have to be purchased. Field hands were valued at from six hundred to one thousand dollars each, but the old men and women and young children would reduce the average price. This would have absorbed $500,000,000, a sum that, prior to the experience of one year's war expenditure, would have appeared staggering. When, however, Mr. Lincoln called attention to the rapidly growing national debt, with no prospect of ending the conflict for years to come, he exclaimed:

"What a splendid investment it would have been!"

These words, as the mentally distressed Lincoln uttered them in that dark hour of the Civil War, were of thrilling import. He rose to his full height;

my eyes instinctively traced his majestic length from his slippers to his head of iron-gray hair, and there was an expression of sadness in his face that I shall never forget.

Referring to the severe criticisms that were launched against him respecting the views he entertained about the reconstruction of the Union, he said:

"I do the best I can, and I mean to keep doing so until the end. If the end brings me out all right, what is said against me won't amount to anything. If the end bring me out wrong, ten angels swearing I was right would make no difference."

The entrance of a delegation prevented a continuance of the conversation. Years afterward, Col. A. K. McClure told me that as late as August, prior to the November elections of 1864, President Lincoln had recurred to his plan for freeing the negroes by purchase, and settling the war on the basis of universal extinction of slavery in all States of the Union at an expense of $400,000,000, a compromise which he believed the Southern leaders, in their hopeless condition after the battle of Gettysburg, would be glad to accept. Mr. Lincoln went on to predict that the promulgation of such a scheme at that time would defeat his re-election. McClure not only confirmed him in that opinion, but added that Congress was in no mood to appropriate so large a sum of money.

Redemption of these bonds, if the Union was restored after the war, would fall in part on the Southern people; they would be paying out of their own pockets for the liberation of their slaves. This statement of McClure's is remarkable because it indicates that Lincoln believed that the *status quo ante bellum* could be restored and reconstruction formalities avoided. Unfortunately, under Andrew Johnson, who succeeded to the Presidency after Lincoln's assassination, and subsequently under President Hayes, the "carpet-bag" régime, with all its horrors and corruption, was inflicted upon the Southern States.

Colonel McClure's judgment was keen and accurate. Congress, led by Senator Sumner and Representatives Thaddeus Stevens and Henry Winter Davis, would have repudiated such a proposition if made by Lincoln. Even after his re-election he could not have secured the money for that purpose.

Mr. Carpenter, who made the famous painting of the Cabinet when Mr. Lincoln read the draft of the Emancipation Proclamation, and who was a client of mine, told me Mr. Lincoln had said to him that for a long time he had been considering the necessity of eventually issuing the Proclamation; but that he was held back by the intense desire that was always in his mind to restore the

Union, and his fear that if he proclaimed emancipation prematurely the restoration of the Union would be prevented. During his entire administration and in all his addresses this desire to restore the Union was supreme and it controlled his every action.

On the momentous occasion when Lincoln read the preliminary draft of his Emancipation Proclamation before his Cabinet, he amused himself and the others—with the exception of Secretary Stanton, who was plainly amazed at the President's seeming levity—by first reading to them from Artemas Ward's amusing story of "The High-Handed Outrage at Utica."

Later on I remember having been present when Lincoln said, "If my name is ever remembered it will be for this act; my whole soul is in it."

It is curious, the thing we call history. An act popularly regarded as madness at one period is hailed as concrete wisdom at another. History is only a crystallization of popular beliefs.

Many people very close to Lincoln have doubted his sympathy for the slaves, and have referred to his frequent characterization of abolitionists as "a disturbing element in the nation, that ought to be subjected to some sort of control." They assert that his efforts were directed solely to restraining the ambitions of the slaveholders to extend their system of human bondage over larger areas of the United States.

Such judgment of Lincoln is at variance with my personal observations and does him a grave injustice. His nature was essentially sympathetic, although he never went the length of asserting that he regarded the black man as his social equal.

Subsequent observation has shown me that the immediate admission of the liberated slaves to equal rights of franchise was an error.

It revived the former bitterness with which the Southern people had regarded the Northerners, and imposed a grievous injustice upon them, an injustice naturally and forcibly resented. And so followed the formation of the "Invisible Empire" and the excesses of the "Ku-Klux Klan."

## VIII
# The Renomination

The renomination of Mr. Lincoln in 1864 was not
accomplished with ease. The difficulties did not all
show upon the surface, because some of the President's closest associates were secretly conspiring
against him. Open and frank opposition came
from such influential Republicans as Henry Winter Davis, of Maryland, Benjamin F. Wade, of
Ohio, and Horace Greeley, of New York, who
believed his re-election impossible. But the opposition of Salmon P. Chase, of Ohio, was secret, as he
had been scheming for the nomination himself.
Chase, while regarding himself as Mr. Lincoln's
friend and constantly protesting his friendship to
the President, held a condescending opinion of
Mr. Lincoln's intellect. He could not believe the
people so blind as to prefer Abraham Lincoln to
Salmon Chase. He vigorously protested, both ver-
bally and in letters written to every part of the
country, his indifference to the Presidency, at the

same time painting pessimistically the dreadful state of government affairs, and indicating, not always subtly, his willingness to accept the nomination.

As to Chase's candidacy, Lincoln once said, according to Nicolay: "I have determined to shut my eyes as far as possible to everything of the sort. Mr. Chase makes a good secretary and I shall keep him where he is." Then with characteristic magnanimity, he added: "If Chase becomes President, all right. I hope we may never have a worse man." But as Joseph Medill, editor of the Chicago *Tribune,* wrote in December, 1863:

> I presume it is true that Mr. Chase's friends are making for his nomination, but it is all lost labor; Old Abe has the inside tracke so completely that he will be nominated by acclamation when the convention meets.

A reference here to the activities of Chase's brilliant daughter, Kate Chase Sprague, in the Tilden and Hayes contest many years later, may be pardoned. It is well known that through her potent influence the contest was finally decided in favor of Rutherford B. Hayes, and against Samuel J. Tilden. This influence, it has been said, was used in a spirit of revenge against Mr. Tilden for defeating her father for the Democratic nomination in 1868. Col. A. K. McClure agrees with me in this, as will be shown by the following quotation from his book, *Our Presidents and How We Make Them:*

The Democratic National Convention met in New York on the 4th of July, 1868. There was a strong sentiment among the delegates favorable to the nomination of a liberal Republican for President, but Chief-Justice Chase, who was an old-time Democrat and who had won a very large measure of Democratic confidence by his ruling in the impeachment case of President Johnson, was a favorite with a very powerful circle of friends who had quietly, but very thoroughly, as they believed, organized to have him nominated by a spontaneous tidal wave after a protracted deadlock between the leading candidates. Chase would have been nominated at the time Seymour was chosen, and in like manner, had it not been for the carefully laid plan of Samuel J. Tilden to prevent the success of Chase. Tilden was a master leader, subtle as he was able, and he thoroughly organized the plan to nominate Seymour, not so much that he desired Seymour, but because he was implacable in his hostility to Chase.

It was well known by Chase and his friends that Tilden crucified Chase in the Democratic convention of 1868, and this act of Tilden's had an impressive sequel eight years later when the election of Tilden hung in the balance in the Senate, and when Kate Chase Sprague, the accomplished daughter of Chase, decided the battle against Tilden.

While Charles Sumner was openly for Lincoln, he privately criticized him, even after the promulgation of the Emancipation Proclamation which had freed the slaves of the South.

I have always believed that Lincoln did not consult with Sumner as to that message, and that that was the cause of his ill-feeling. Thaddeus Stevens, the great Free Soil representative of Pennsylvania, was dissatisfied because the President was unwilling to confiscate all the property of the secessionists and to inflict other punishments upon them: he was openly hostile to Lincoln.

For the following hitherto unpublished letter, from Horace Greeley to Mark Howard, a prominent Connecticut Republican, I am indebted to the latter's daughter, Mrs. Graves. It throws an interesting light upon the fears and uncertainties of the period, and indicates Greeley's lack of confidence in Lincoln as the strong man of the nation. The letter is dated ten months before the second election, and Greeley's opposition to Mr. Lincoln's renomination became the more undisguised and intense as time went on.

OFFICE OF THE TRIBUNE.
NEW YORK, *Jan. 10, 1864.*

DEAR SIR,—I mean to keep the Presidency in the background until we see whether we cannot close up the war. I am terribly afraid of letting the war run into the next Presidential term; I fear it will prove disastrous to go to the ballot-boxes with the war still pending. Let us have peace first, then we can see into the future.

Yours,
HORACE GREELEY.

MARCH HOWARD, ESQ.,
    Hartford, Conn.

Horace Greeley gave open expression to his opposition in the New York *Tribune,* Friday, April 29, 1864.

In this issue Mr. Greeley, referring to the statement of the President, "I claim not to have controlled events, but confess plainly that events have controlled me," declared that "had he been a little more docile to their teaching and prompt to apprehend their bearing we should have been saved many diasters and rivers of precious blood. May we hope that with regard to the murder of our soldiers who have surrendered, and other questions of the hour, he will have learned something from the sore experience of the past?"

Other newspapers joined the *Tribune* in opposing Lincoln's renomination, as witness these excerpts from the New York *Herald,* August 6, 1864:

Senator Wade, of Ohio, and Representative Davis, of Maryland, Chairman of the Senate and House Committees on the rebellious States prepared and presented in their official capacity an indictment against Abraham Lincoln, the executive head of the nation, and the nominee of his party for another term of office, charging him with arrogance, ignorance, usurpation, knavery, and a host of other deadly sins including that of hostility to the rights of humanity and to the principles of republican government.

Mr. Lincoln has been frequently represented as entertaining and expressing an ardent wish that he could slip off his shoulders the anxieties and labors belonging to his present position and place upon them the musket and knapsack of a Union volunteer. The opportunity of realizing that wish now presents itself. The country would be overjoyed to see it realized, and all the people would say "Amen" to it. Let him make up his mind to join the quota which his town of Springfield, Ill., will next be called on to furnish. He is said to have done well as railsplitter, and we have no doubt that he will do equally well as a soldier. As a President of the United States he must have sense enough to see and acknowledge he has been an egregious failure. The best thing he can do now for himself, his party, and his country is to retire from the high position to which, in an evil hour, he was exalted.

One thing must be self-evident to him, and that is that under no circumstances can he hope to be the next President of the United States, and if he will only make a virtue of necessity and withdraw from the Presidential campaign . . .

In the New York *Tribune,* August 24, 1864, under the heading, "Copperhead Treason," the *Daily News* is quoted as referring to President Lincoln as "our intriguing chief magistrate."

Finally, there was general disaffection, centering largely in New York and St. Louis, and a so-called convention of opponents of Lincoln gathered at Cleveland in May, and indulged in denunciation of Lincoln, which included a bitter letter from Wendell Phillips. This self-styled "radical Democracy" adopted a platform, nominated Fremont, and practically disappeared.

The patriotic and self-sacrificing people of the North were almost a unit in sustaining President Lincoln, and, by sheer force of numbers, swept aside the ungrateful or designing Republican leaders who would have defeated the great emancipator.

During the days that immediately preceded his

renomination, Mr. Lincoln gave way to despondency, and, although he never said so in words, one could clearly see by the anxiety he manifested that he was sorely perplexed to account for the animus of certain men against him. He appeared to be especially anxious about New York, and to fear that the enmity of Seward's old friends and the hostility of Mr. Greeley might cause him to lose the delegation from the Empire State. I was in Washington at that time on professional business, and was able to impart to him positive information regarding his strength in various parts of the State. To his inquiry about the situation in New York, I told him that, while Greeley was still in the sulks, yet I thought Seward and Weed were coming around to him (Lincoln) handsomely, and that their action would undoubtedly influence the Seward partisans. I added that in my opinion Greeley would before long forget his disappointment and fall into line. Mr. Lincoln listened attentively and nodded assent. "That's good news," he said, heartily, seemingly well pleased with my prognostications.

Col. A. K. McClure, of Pennsylvania, stood very close to the President at this time and did not disguise from him the treachery of several Republican leaders.

Anxiety had become an obsession with the President. This seemed due to a physical and mental reaction after three years of incessant worry and strain, And yet at this hour General Grant appeared to be smashing his way through the Wilderness, toward Richmond; General Sherman had left Chattanooga on his march to the sea by which the Confederacy was cut in two; the dashing Sheridan was harassing the enemy in the Shenandoah Valley, and the collapse of the rebellion was foreshadowed.

I am sure Mr. Lincoln cared but little for his own political future, but he was most desirous of carrying out his plans regarding reconstruction, and the frankness with which he had spoken his views on the subject made enemies of such men as Greeley, Sumner, and Stevens. Had he dissembled, concealing his sympathies for the suffering civilian population in the South who had taken no active part in the rebellion, until such time as he could properly lay his plans before Congress and explain them, hostility against him would have been confined to a few politicians actuated by envy or personal ambition.

But Mr. Lincoln made no secret of his desire for the prompt reorganization of the seceded States, immediately peace was attained; and for their readmission into the Union, with representation in both Houses of Congress, thus carrying out the thought always uppermost in his mind of the restoration of the Union. And yet his sorrows, worriments, and perplexities could not drown his sense of humor, as the following occurrence shows:

A conference was held on shipboard in Hampton Roads about the time that the collapse of the Confederacy seemed imminent, the consultants including the Vice-President of the Confederacy, Alexander H. Stevens, and R. M. T. Hunter and J. A. Campbell, on the one side, and Mr. Lincoln and Mr. Seward on the other.

Mr. Hunter, to enforce his contentions, referred to the correspondence between Charles the First, of England, and Parliament.

"Mr. Lincoln's face," it is reported, "wore the inscrutable expression which generally preceded his hardest hits," as he replied: "Upon questions of history I must refer you to Mr. Seward, for he is posted in such things, and I do not profess to be; my only distinct recollection of the matter is that Charles lost his head."

Under the reconstruction policy planned by the great President and carried out by his successor, President Johnson, the rebel States were taken back in the Union with the same representation in Congress they had before they started on the war of secession.

To obviate the danger which would arise from

the control of the Southern States by the unrepentant rebels, and to minimize the danger that might result from the large number of members they would have in Congress, it was deemed necessary to give the illiterate and shiftless negroes, just emerging from slavery, and who constituted a majority of the voters in many of the Southern States, the right to vote.

This resulted in the detestable State governments composed of negroes and "carpet-bag" whites, no less corrupt than the negroes. The whites were called "carpet-baggers," because they came from the North, with no intention of remaining permanently; they only wanted to exploit the south for their own profit; and they generally traveled in light marching order, with all their worldly possessions packed in the familiar carpet-bag of the period.

Sumner, Stevens, and Winter Davis opposed this reconstruction policy, contending that the rebel States should be held as conquered territory until a new generation should arrive on the scene.

I did not hesitate to say at the time that they were right. Had their policy been adopted the terrible evils of the "carpet-bag" governments would have been avoided.

In the last conversation I had with Mr. Lincoln on the subject of his renomination, about ten days before the convention of 1864, I tried to convince him that his doubts and fears were unwarranted, but I did not succeed in lightening the gloom. He probably thought me too young a man to form an accurate opinion, but I had investigated for myself, as well as advised with the best-informed Republicans in my State. It seemed as though he could not forget that previous miraculous nomination by a convention in which two-thirds of the delegates favored another candidate; he feared lest now the boot might be on the other leg.

The Republican National Convention assembled at Baltimore on June 7, 1864, the aged Rev. Dr. Robert J. Breckinridge, of Kentucky, being temporary chairman, and ex-Governor William Dennison, of Ohio, permanent presiding officer.

All opposition melted away when the platform was read and adopted. The third plank therein denounced "slavery as the cause of the rebellion, always and everywhere hostile to principles of republican government; therefore, national safety demands its utter and complete extirpation from the soil of the Republic."

Mr. Lincoln was renominated on the first ballot, receiving the unanimous vote of every State, with the exception of Missouri, the delegation from which State was instructed for General Grant. The Missouri vote was at once changed to Lincoln, making the nomination unanimous.

At that convention I circulated among the representatives from other States, and overheard many mutterings of dissatisfaction at the inevitability of the choice, but not a hostile word was spoken from the rostrum. I joined with delegates from my State in addressing a message of congratulation to Mr. Lincoln at Washington.

Greeley, of course, was obliged to come around to support Lincoln's re-election, but he could not refrain from damning him with faint praise.

Under the caption of "Opening the Presidential Campaign," Mr. Greeley, in the *Tribune* of February 23, 1864, thus indicated his change of front toward Mr. Lincoln:

> He has been patriotic, honest, and faithful. He has done his utmost to serve and save the country. . . . He is not infallible, not a genius, not one of those rare, great men who mould their age into the similitude of their own high character, massive abilities, and lofty aims. But, considering his antecedents and his experience of public affairs we are sure the verdict of history in his case will be "well done, thou good and faithful servant." The luster of his good deeds will far outlive the memory of his mistakes and faults.

Perhaps Greeley stood too close to his subject, but surely these condescending words may be considered a masterpiece of ineptitude.

Nor was Mr. Greeley averse to reprinting hostile criticisms from outside sources, as the following excerpts will witness:

In the New York *Tribune,* June 21, 1864, under the heading, "Rebel Views of our Nomination—A Railsplitter and a Tailor," the Richmond *Examiner* is quoted as saying:

> The Convention of Black Republicans in Baltimore have nominated for President of their country Abraham Lincoln, the Illinois railsplitter.
>
> The great army of contractors and office-holders—in short, those who live by war and on the country—have succeeded, at least, in starting Lincoln fairly for another race. It amounts to a declaration that those conventioners desire to see four years more in all respects like unto the last four years.

Another extract from the Richmond *Examiner* also appears in the *Tribune* at about the same date:

> The only merit we can discover in this Baltimore ticket is the merit of *consistency;* it is all of a piece; the tail does not shame the head, nor the head shame the tail. A railsplitting buffoon and a boorish tailor, both from the backwoods. Both growing up in uncouth ignorance, they would afford a grotesque subject for a satiric poet.

I had known from the President's own lips, at my last interview, that he desired the selection of Andrew Johnson, a Tennessean, whose steadfast support of the Federal cause in these troublesome times had attracted attention. I was not in sympathy with that plan, because I thought that Johnson would cost the party many votes among the radicals in New England.

Nobody could forecast at that time with reasonable uncertainty the Democratic candidates, and there was considerable fear that General Grant might be named. He was popularly believed to be bringing the rebellion to an early finish; if he succeeded in forcing the capitulation of General Lee before the Democratic convention met in Chicago at the end of August, the opposition party might seize upon him and could probably elect him. Grant had been an old-line Democrat and, so far as known, had voted for Douglas in 1860. There was no political reason why Grant could not accept such a nomination.

In June, General McClellan's name had not been seriously considered. He was a man with a grievance, for he had been removed from the command of the Federal Army after a long endurance of his procrastinating policy by the administration. The universal affection felt for McClellan throughout the Northern Army, especially the Army of the Potomac, seems difficult of explanation.

# IX

# The Campaign of 1864

The campaign for the Republican ticket began before the name of the Democratic candidate was known. Speakers were haranguing the people in every Northern State, but if Mr. Lincoln's doubts about his renomination had been serious, his fear of defeat at the polls developed into a veritable mental panic. Both Nicolay and Gideon Welles refer to the following note, which, indorsed on the back by all the Cabinet members, was sealed and committed to the keeping of the Secretary of the Navy, with instructions that it should not be opened until after election. I believe that the original has been presented by Miss Nicolay to the Library of Congress:

This morning, as for some days past, it seemed improbable that this administration will be re-elected. Then it will be my duty to co-operate with the President-elect so as to save the Union between the election and the inauguration, as my successor will have secured his election on such grounds that he cannot possibly save it afterwards.

*August 23, 1864.*                              A. Lincoln.

It will be seen that this remarkable document bears date six days before the assembling of the Democratic convention at Chicago, on August 29. At that time Mr. Lincoln was aware of the plan to nominate McClellan, and feared his strength.

In the interval between the Republican convention, early in June, and the gathering of the Democrats at the end of August, the progress of the Federal arms had not realized expectations. Grant had not taken Richmond, and Sherman had not administered a decisive blow to General Johnson.

Politically, the situation was somewhat more hopeful. The selection of Andrew Johnson as Vice-President on the Republican ticket had conciliated many Northern Democrats like Judge Holt, General Dix, and General Butler; moreover, it had prevented recognition of the Confederacy by France and England. Lincoln's foresight in substituting the Tennessean for Hannibal Hamlin, of Maine, was generally admitted.

McClellan developed more strength than was suspected. The best opinion is that, had the election occurred directly after his nomination and before people had had opportunity to study the platform upon which he had consented to stand, he would have been successful. Soon after the Democratic convention adjourned, however, the capture of Atlanta by Sherman was announced;

then followed the sturdy blows of Grant at the Confederate capital and Sheridan's series of victories in the Shenandoah Valley. These happy events completely changed the political attitude of the country.

The Democratic managers at Chicago had committed the execrable blunder of declaring in their platform that the war had been a failure and that the public welfare demanded "an immediate effort be made for a cessation of hostilities, with a view to an ultimate convention of all the States."

Little more than two months remained before election day in November, and every speaker that could be commandeered was put into active service. Lincoln himself took no active part in the campaign outside of a few addresses to soldiers, but mass-meetings were held every day and night of the week, and popular preachers with Republican sympathies filled their discourses with appeals in behalf of Lincoln and the necessity of his re-election for the preservation of the Union. Henry Ward Beecher became a tower of strength to the Lincoln cause, and in and out of Plymouth pulpit he advocated the duty of sustaining the administration that had already saved the Union and must ultimately put down the rebellion. I addressed meetings every night.

The campaign soon became one of great acrimony on both sides. Night and day, without cessation, young men like myself, in halls, upon street corners, and from cart-tails, were haranguing, pleading, sermonizing, orating, arguing, extolling our cause and our candidate, and denouncing our opponents. A deal of oratory, elocution, rhetoric, declamation, and eloquence was hurled into the troubled air by speakers on both sides.

Denunciation of Lincoln by Democratic spell-binders was of the bitterest character. Newspapers affiliated with the anti-war party criticized every act of the administration and belittled the conduct of the war by Federal generals in the field. Therefore, Republican speakers did not mince words in criticism of the Democratic Presidential candidate, Gen. George B. McClellan.

On September 27, five weeks before election day, I spoke to an audience that filled every seat in Cooper Institute, on the questions of the hour. Read in the calmness of to-day my language appears unwarrantedly aggressive, but at that time it seemed conservative. As an example of the spirit of the campaign I venture to quote a few extracts:

The battle that will be fought in November between the Union and the Confederate forces north of the Potomac will end in the destruction or exhaustion of the Southern Confederacy. Abraham Lincoln is the commander of the Union forces. I will now prove that George B. McClellan is the leader of the Confederate forces.

While at the head of the Army, McClelland attempted to dictate to President Lincoln a policy acceptable to the Confederate South. Every man in the North influenced by "Copperheads," who opposed the war, demanded that this "fighting general" be replaced at the head of our armies. He had become harnessed to the slave power, and he, with General Pendleton, candidate for Vice-President, became the incarnation of the Democratic peace platform.

McClellan's nomination was received with enthusiasm and cheers by the Confederate soldiers; the Southern newspapers declared that McClellan's election would be helped by Grant's defeat in the field. Confederate bonds advanced on the announcement of McClellan's nomination. Every Southern sympathizer in the North, passive or active in his devotion to Jefferson Davis, will vote for McClellan.

He says in his letter of acceptance that his sentiments are identical with those of the platform which pronounced the war a failure, and he promised, if the Democratic candidate were elected, an immediate cessation of hostilities.

I called attention to the fact that such men as Fernando Wood, Vallandigham, and Horatio Seymour, once Governor of New York, supported McClellan, thus indorsing the letter of acceptance, in which he promises to enforce the policy set forth in the peace platform of his party.

McClellan's military career, consistent with his whole history, may be summed up in one word—"delay"—which gave to the Confederacy what it needed—time. Is it not then true that McClellan heads, in this campaign, the Confederate forces North?

I then read the following excerpt from the Democratic platform:

Resolved, that this Convention does explicitly declare, as the sense of the American people, that after four years of failure to restore the Union by the experiment of war during which, under the pretense of a military necessity for a war-power higher than the Constitution, the Constitution itself has been disregarded in every part; and public liberty and private right alike trodden down, and the material prosperity of the country essentially impaired, justice, humanity, liberty, and the public welfare demand that immediate efforts be made for the cessation of hostilities, with a view to the ultimate convention of the States or other peaceful means, to the end that at the earliest practicable moment peace may be restored on the basis of Federal Union of the States. Resolved, that the direct interference of the military authorities of the United States in the recent elections held in Kentucky, Maryland, Missouri, and Delaware was a shameful violation of the Constitution and a repetition of such acts in the approaching election will be held as revolutionary and resisted with all the means and power under our control.

In other words [I resumed], it was a bold and pernicious declaration of hostilities that war should close at once and that a convention should be called at a later period, to revise the Constitution. But it is easy to comprehend that when such a convention should be called, Jefferson Davis would refuse to enter its doors, and be prepared to enforce his refusal.

Jefferson Davis, his resources crippled and with his last levies on the firing-line, is naturally anxious that Lincoln be defeated, for he knows, by this time, that with Lincoln as President the Confederacy will be compelled to abandon a hopeless contest. Davis cannot, and will not, continue the fight if Lincoln is re-elected, notwithstanding his threat to "fight to the last ditch."

Lincoln's re-election will banish all hope of triumph for the Confederacy. A firm and everlasting peace will follow, based upon a reconstructed Union and freedom everywhere. The

American Union, strong, powerful, and freed from slavery, will be honored the world over.

> "Be it storm, or summer weather,
>     Peaceful calm or battle jar,
> Stand in beauteous strength together,
>     Sister States as once ye were."

Large sums of money were expended in expensive printing during that campaign. Some of the publications were elaborately designed and illustrated. Recently one of the Lincoln and Johnson posters has been presented to me, and the miniature reproduction on the following page should be of interest.

The names of the electors for the State of New York include that of the writer. The poster is printed in several colors, it is five feet high and three and one-half feet wide. It is in a perfect state of preservation.

As I have indicated, the victories of Sheridan and Sherman produced a revulsion against peace sentiment throughout the North that literally swamped McClellan. The popular vote was large, Lincoln securing 2,213,665 votes, and McClellan 1,802,237 votes. Except among the troops from Pennsylvania and Kentucky, the soldier vote was overwhelmingly in favor of Lincoln. This was a surprise.

It is interesting to illustrate the growth of our

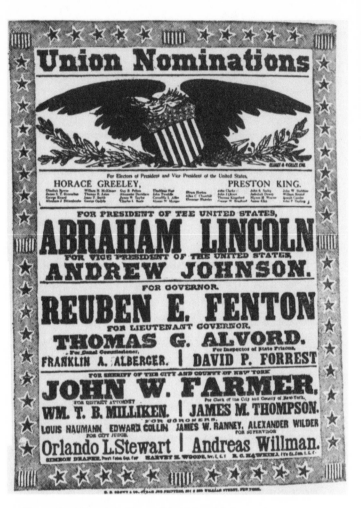

Poster for Lincoln's Second Presidential Campaign.

country by a comparison with the popular vote of 1912 when Wilson received 6,291,776 votes, Taft 3,481,119, and Roosevelt 4,106,247.

Of the electoral votes, Lincoln received 212, and McClellan only 21. Until the defeat of Mr. Taft by Woodrow Wilson in 1912, this was a record of defeat. In the latter year Mr. Wilson received 435 votes, Mr. Taft 15, and Mr. Roosevelt 81.

The electoral ticket for Lincoln having been successful in New York State, the thirty-three electors, of whom I was one, met at Albany and cast the votes of the State for Abraham Lincoln and Andrew Johnson.

The ballots were inscribed on wooden blocks, and read as follows:

President, Abraham Lincoln

and underneath, in brackets,

[Abram J. Dittenhoefer] Elector

A few weeks later I took one of these wooden block ballots with me to Washington and showed it to the President. He asked me if I would not give it to him as a souvenir, which I was very glad to do.

Horace Greeley and Preston King were the two electors-at-large. Although Greeley had violently opposed the renomination of Lincoln, wise counsels put him at the head of the Presidential electors, a compliment that Mr. Greeley told me highly gratified him, in view of his previous attitude toward the President.

When Mr. Greeley became the Democratic candidate for President in 1872 and many Republicans seceded from the Republican party, Mr. Greeley requested me to act as chairman of the executive committee of the Liberal Republican Central Committee in New York City, and I consented to do so. Chauncey M. Depew, who also identified himself with the Liberal Republican organization, became the candidate of the party for Secretary of State of New York. I afterward regretted that I had joined in that movement, and my regret was intensified when Greeley's campaign turned out to be so great a fiasco.

Lincoln's assassination, April 12, 1865, thwarted the generous, noble-hearted plans which he had devised for the restoration of the Union, and resulted in imposing upon the Southern people by Andrew Johnson, Lincoln's successor, the corrupt "carpet-bag" régime.

Lincoln's place in the history of civilization is immutably fixed. During the last ten years of his career, he was the greatest of all living men. As statesman and reformer he belongs not alone to America, but to the whole world.

George Washington established this Republic, but the curse of human slavery adhered to the otherwise splendid Government he was so largely instrumental in creating.

Abraham Lincoln eradicated this curse.

Halleck's verse comes back to me again as I close these recollections:

One of the few, the immortal names
    That were not born to die!